THE
TAMING
OF THE
SCREW

The best cartoons from *Do it yourself* magazine

BILL THACKER

BLANDFORD PRESS
POOLE · DORSET

First published in the U.K. 1984 by
Blandford Press, Link House, West Street,
Poole, Dorset BH15 1LL

Reprinted 1984

Copyright © 1984 *Do It Yourself Magazine,*
Link House Magazines (Croydon) Ltd,
Link House, Dingwall Avenue, Croydon CR9 2TA

Distributed in the United States by Sterling Publishing
Publishing Co., Inc., 2 Park Avenue, New York, N.Y.
10016, U.S.A.

ISBN 0 7173 1457 3

Printed and bound in Great Britain by Purnell & Sons
(Book Production) Ltd., Member of the BPCC Group,
Paulton, Bristol

BUILDERS SUPPLIES

'Mortar? Yessir. . . cement, lime, or shell-throwing?'

ZUBOTOLAND MISSIONARY EXPEDITION

'Could bwana advise on loft conversion?'

. . . more obstinate tree stumps often require more intensive means of removal. . .

. . .never underestimate the fixing
power of modern materials. . .

TODAY'S PRICE OF GOLD £38.80 PER OZ.

HARDWAR[E]

GOLD ENAMEL 4 OZ. TINS £156 EACH (+ VAT)

CEYLON TEA

'You'll find this hard to believe, but I built this garage *entirely* from scrap materials.'

HOW TO TACKLE RISING DAMP

'And *now* we have *falling* damp'

. . .the enthusiasm for DIY home improvement should be tempered with considerations of local building styles. . .

'Could you cut this down to a tenon saw?'

'*Fait accompli?* No, mate. . . it's a power sub-station'

'. . .and anyway, chicken wire is much *cheaper* than a shotgun'

'So my nephew was right. . . the problem's a choked pilot jet'

'I promise to mend the roof, the whole roof, and nothing but the roof'

'Would you kindly not leave
food stains on the tiles?'

'We've hit the Bakerloo Line, Guv'

'Well I *did* get the taps off the basin!'

. . .the DIY plumber should always be wary of local variations in water pressure. . .

'I've bought that record you like so much. . . *The Stripper*'

'*Ah!* The Hanging Judge!'

'My husband's work. . .
he's very clever with his hands'

'For your last redecorating, 5 rolls paper,
3 pints paint, dated 8th May 1946'

HOUSHO INSURANCE LTD

QUOTATIONS FREE

CHECK IT YOURSELF CALCULATOR

£9.95 AVAILABLE AT COUNTER

CAR INSURANCE IMMEDIATE COVER

PRICE LIST

ROLD CARAVANS LTD

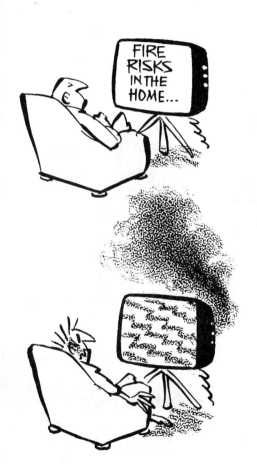

'Our roof is now ventilated. . . this is rainwater'

'One thing about this way of life, Arnold. . . no central heating problems'

'It says here that ladders *must* be stored *horizontally*'

'How's the . . . *atishoo* . . . the
arashoo . . . the sanding going?'

'*Somebody* has been using my
mortarboard *as* a mortarboard'

'Lady wants an 8 × 4ft *clipboard!*'

...and the argument that DIY
takes away jobs is, of course,
open to debate...

'Cut out the blister with a
hammer and cold chisel. . .

. . .good gracious! Daphne's fainted!'

'Forty-seven are back from their holiday. . .
I just heard their cistern flush'

'Ah! The return of the native'

'Good tip in here for economising on my paint brush cleanser which you keep borrowing'

'Sorry, Miss . . . purely maintenance, I assure you'

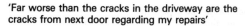

'Far worse than the cracks in the driveway are the cracks from next door regarding my repairs'

'The brush I borrowed last June'

'If you'd kindly fit an even longer lead, perhaps
I could borrow the saw sometime'

'There's a washing machine salesman at the door. Should I send him away, or what. . .?'

'Lukewarm! The fools haven't adjusted the lockshield valve. . . I'll nip back to the car and get me a screwdriver'

'Don't worry about the durability of that paint. . . we'll be moving house very soon'

'The final cure for that condensation. . . we'll move to another house'

'A man smelling strongly of sewage is seeking legal advice on drain responsibilities'

'My husband's suggested cure for this musty smell was a clothes peg per person'

'I shall need a seven foot fence, as my neighbour is six feet five inches tall'

'George! It's the new local Smoke Control Officer'

'It's not *all* damp, sir. . . the rot for instance is all dry''

'One consolation however, is that the fungus in your cellar is edible'

ESTATE AGENT

HEALTH OFFICER

'Ah! That chap downstairs finally got the capstan off his tap'

'So. . . *another* 24 hours delay whilst you soak the brushes!'

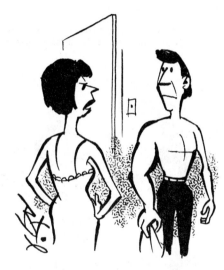

'But surely you could use *both* arms for all that polishing?'

'Jim says magnetic North has moved two degrees since you took all those nails out'

'*Now* it's a suspended ceiling. . . George has gone to a cricket match'

'The 24 hours is up
Harold. . . time to lightly
sand the surface again'

'Edward's window frames are in such appalling taste,
even the woodworm has moved elsewhere'

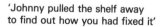

'Johnny pulled the shelf away
to find out how you had fixed it'

'That night on the tiles I promised you. . .'

'Yet another use for that marvellous adhesive tape'

'The idea surely was to make carpet *squares*, not carpet *rhomboids*'

MISSING PERSONS BUREAU

'Well, he said he was going to frost some glass, and the next thing I had was a postcard from Reykjavik'

'That reminds me – I must paint that old corrugated iron'

'A bit late, thinking of protecting them, now that they're all extinct species'

'Our garage floor is so *oily*, we wonder why the OPC countries haven't made a bid for it'

'Repainting the wall took 18 hours, including 1½ hours writing to *Do It Yourself* about it'

'You just *will not* buy British!'

'Forgot to tell you, doll. . .' I've freed the sticking door'

'Now I've finished this split driveway, my wife wants to get a three-wheeled car'

'Sharpen them? Surely you have to blunt them first?'

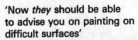

'Now *they* should be able to advise you on painting on difficult surfaces'

'My wife's a bit of a prude . . .she prefers the term "Paint *remover*" to "Paint *stripper*"'

. . .the general feeling that estate agents tend to over-glamorise their properties has no basis in fact. . .

'The olde worlde character has been preserved, right down to the rubber-covered wiring. . .'

'Henshaw's had a bad day. . . his planning application was turned down, and his mother-in-law has turned up'

'Once the bedroom's nice and warm you'll have one *less* excuse for staying out all night'

'I do wish I could fit your mother with some sort of non-return valve'

'Ahem. . . I thought I said we needed a *partition*'

'Yes, it does look rather nice. Unfortunately, we had to glue all the books in place'

'The City Council *did* make us a house-improvement
grant, dear. . . meet Jennifer Grant'

'Fat lot of good, *us* having a picture
window, with a sewage farm right opposite'

. . .and, of course, DIY enthusiasm need not stop at the garage door. . .

'*Great* idea, decorating in puce, green and magenta. . . we haven't had one visitor since!'